ALL ABOUT ANIMALS IN THE SEA

All About Sea Otters

Kerrily Sapet

EZ READERS
AN IMPRINT OF MITCHELL LANE PUBLISHERS

CREATING YOUNG NONFICTION READERS

EZ Readers offer nonfiction for beginning readers in PreK through first grade, using simple language, clear illustrations, and engaging facts to build vocabulary and confidence.

TIPS FOR READING NONFICTION WITH BEGINNING READERS

Talk about Nonfiction

Begin by explaining that nonfiction books give us information that is true. The book will be organized around a specific topic or idea, and we may learn new facts through reading.

Look at the Parts

Most nonfiction books have helpful features. Our *EZ Readers* include color photographs and graphic aids, a table of contents, a glossary, and an index. Share the purpose of these features with your reader.

Color Photos and Graphic Aids

A lot of information can be found by "reading" photos, charts, maps, and other graphic aids found within nonfiction texts. Help your reader learn more about the different ways information can be displayed.

Table of Contents

Located at the front of the book, this list shows the big ideas within the text and the page numbers where they can be found.

Glossary

Located at the back of the book, the glossary defines key words and phrases that are related to the topic. These words and phrases can be found in the text in colored type.

Index

Located at the back of the book, an index is an alphabetical list of topics and the page numbers where they can be found.

With a little help and guidance about reading nonfiction, you can feel good about introducing a young reader to the world of *EZ Readers* nonfiction books.

EZ Readers is an imprint of:

Mitchell Lane PUBLISHERS

2001 SW 31st Avenue
Hallandale, FL 33009
mitchelllanepub.com

First Edition, 2026.

Author: Kerrily Sapet
Editor: Morgan Brody

ISBN 979-8-89260-839-8 (library binding)
ISBN 979-8-90145-038-3 (paperback)
ISBN 979-8-89260-941-8 (ebook)

LC record available at https://lccn.loc.gov/2025950852

Photo credits: Shutterstock, ROMAN RYBALKO, cover, 1; Shutterstock, Northern Owl, cover, 1, 2, 3, 4, 8, 15, 18; Shutterstock, KensCanning, cover, 1, 22; Adobe, , 3, 9, 10, 14, 19; Shutterstock, ucchie79, 5; Shutterstock, rbrown10, 6–7; Shutterstock, Karl Weller, 9; Shutterstock, Kris Wiktor, 10–11; Shutterstock, Kris Clifford, 12–13, 22; Shutterstock, Geoff G. Wildlife Photos, 14, 22; Shutterstock, Manuel Balesteri, 19, 22; Shutterstock, EQRoy, 20, 22; Shutterstock, Eric Isselee, 21; Shutterstock, divedog, 22; Shutterstock, Vibe Images, 22; Shutterstock, mikeledray, 22

Table of Contents

Meeting An Ocean Diver

Imagine you are in a kayak. The water is cold. You float near seaweed.

A fluffy round head pokes up from underwater. It has a black nose and whiskers. A sea otter! It is as long as a bathtub and weighs as much as a big dog.

Otter Watching

The sea otter is dark brown. It has webbed feet and a short tail. Its thick fur keeps it warm.

OTTER OBSERVATION!

A sea otter's fur is so thick that its skin never gets wet.

OTTER OBSERVATION!

Sea otters can hold their breath for six minutes.

The otter dives deep underwater. It pops up to breathe. Sea otters are not fish. They are **mammals**, like people. They breathe air.

The otter floats on its back in seaweed called **kelp**. You see more otters nearby. They rest in a group called a **raft**. Some otters link arms to stay together.

OTTER OBSERVATION!

Sea otter teeth are twice as strong as yours. This helps them crunch through the **shells** of their foods.

Looking for Food

You see an otter holding a **sea urchin**. The otter pulls a rock from under its arm. It uses the rock to crack open the sea urchin and eat the meat inside. Other otters are eating fish and clams.

One otter tucks a clam under its arm to save for later. The otters are quiet. You hear one sneeze. Another otter growls.

Where Do Sea Otters Live?

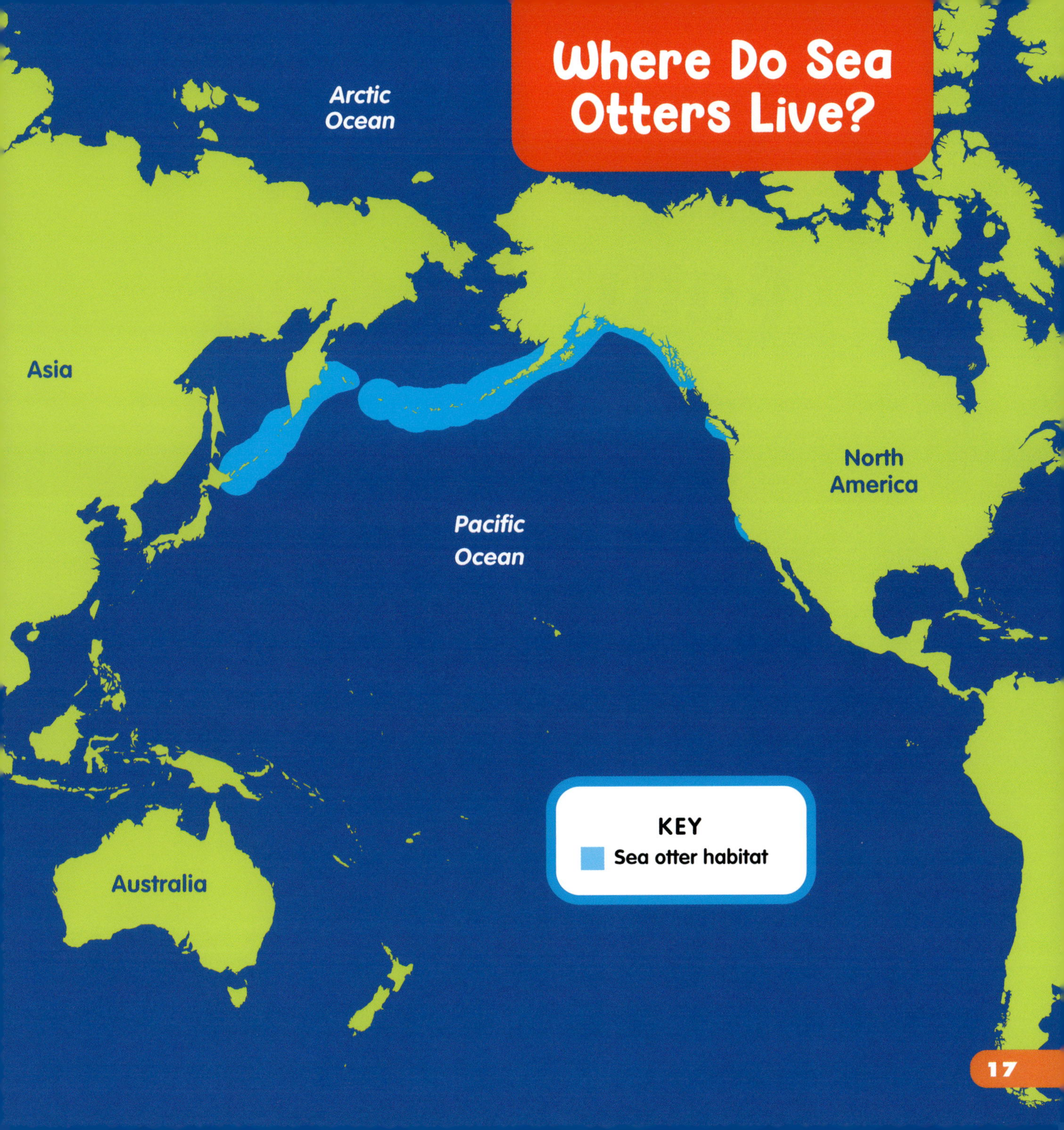

Sea Otter Families and the Future

An otter floats by with a baby on her chest. A baby otter is called a **pup**. A pup is as heavy as 12 apples and as long as two pencils. It drinks its mother's milk.

OTTER OBSERVATION!

Sea otter pups like to wrestle.

Sea otters can live 23 years. **Pollution** harms them. Only a few remain in the wild. Maybe someday you will see a real sea otter.

Parts of a Sea Otter

Fur

Thick hair that keeps a sea otter warm.

Tail

A sea otter uses its strong tail to steer in the water.

Paws

A sea otter has two front paws that it uses like hands to find food, eat, and clean its fur.

Feet

A sea otter has two back feet with webbed toes, like a duck, to help it swim.

Glossary

kelp (KEL-p)
large brown seaweed

mammal (MAM-uhl) an animal that breathes air, has hair, and drinks milk from its mother

pollution (po-LOO-shun) dirty air, land, or water

pup (puhp)
a baby otter

raft (raft)
a group of resting otters

sea urchin (C erchin) an ocean animal that looks like a ball covered in spikes

shell (shel) a hard outer cover that protects an animal

Quiz

1. Are sea otters fish?

A. Yes B. No

2. Do sea otters breathe air?

A. Yes B. No

3. Do sea otters eat whales?

A. Yes B. No

4. Are sea otters babies called pups?

A. Yes B. No

ANSWER KEY:

1. No
2. Yes
3. No
4. Yes

Further Reading

DK. *Sea Otters.* New York, NY: DK Publishing, 2023.

Lim, Angela. *Sea Otter Families.* Mendota Heights, MN: North Star Editions, 2024.

Schwartz, Heather. *Sea Otters: Kelp Forest Engineers.* Minneapolis, MN: Lerner Publishing, 2025.

On the Internet

Sea Otters

https://www.montereybayaquarium.org/visit/exhibits/sea-otters

Meet the sea otters at Monterrey Bay Aquarium.

Sea Otters

https://kids.nationalgeographic.com/animals/mammals/facts/sea-otter

Read fun facts and see pictures of sea otters.

Sea Otters

https://www.sheddaquarium.org/animals/sea-otter

Learn about and watch videos of the sea otters at Shedd Aquarium.

Index

About the Author

Kerrily Sapet has written more than 30 books for kids. She lives near Chicago with her family. When she was ten, she saw sea otters at Shedd Aquarium. She loved watching them zoom through the water. She saw a sea otter in Monterrey Bay when she visited California. Sapet hopes to see a sea otter pup someday.